GUILDING THE NEXT GENERATION

Tips on Giving Effective Advice to Teenagers

Neil S. Reveles

Time of contents

I. Introduction

Importance of guiding the next generation
Overview of the guide
II. Understanding the Next Generation

Characteristics of the current generation of teenagers
Identifying common issues and challenges
III. Effective Communication Strategies

Listening actively to teenagers
Building rapport and trust
Using non-judgmental language
IV. Providing Support and Guidance

Creating a supportive environment
Encouraging healthy habits and positive behaviors

Addressing sensitive issues such as mental health, drugs, and sex
V. Balancing Freedom and Responsibility

Setting boundaries and expectations
Encouraging independence while maintaining guidance
Teaching decision-making skills
VI. Role-Modeling and Leading by Example

Being a positive influence for the next generation
Demonstrating healthy behaviors and values
Encouraging social responsibility and civic engagement
VII. Conclusion

Recap of key points
Final thoughts on guiding the next generation

I. Introduction

Once upon a time, Kate and Kennedy were a young couple who had always dreamed of starting a family. After several years of trying, they were blessed with a beautiful baby girl named Emily.

From the moment Emily was born, Kate and Kennedy were committed to providing her with the best possible upbringing. They knew that they wanted to raise a confident, independent, and ambitious young woman who could achieve her dreams.

As Emily grew up, Kate and Kennedy made sure to provide her with plenty of opportunities to explore her interests and pursue her passions. They enrolled her in dance classes, piano lessons, and sports teams, and encouraged her to try new things and take on challenges.

At the same time, they also instilled in Emily the importance of hard work, perseverance, and a positive attitude. Whenever Emily faced setbacks or obstacles, Kate and Kennedy were there to offer guidance, support, and encouragement.

As Emily entered her teenage years, she began to develop a strong interest in science and technology. Kate and Kennedy recognized this passion and made sure to provide her with resources and opportunities to pursue her interests. They enrolled her in coding classes, encouraged her to participate in robotics competitions, and even helped her build her own computer.

With the support and guidance of her parents, Emily excelled in her studies and went on to pursue a degree in computer science. She landed a job at a tech startup after graduation and quickly made a name for herself in the industry.

Kate and Kennedy were overjoyed to see their daughter achieve her dreams, but they knew that it was Emily's hard work and determination that had gotten her there. They were proud to have played a role in her success, and grateful for the love and support that had helped her become the amazing young woman she was today.

in today's rapidly changing world, the next generation is facing unprecedented challenges and opportunities. As parents, educators, and mentors, it is our responsibility to guide and support these young people as they navigate their way through adolescence and into adulthood.

Guiding the next generation can be a daunting task, particularly as technology and social media continue to shape the way teenagers interact with the world. However, with the right strategies and tools, we can create a supportive environment that empowers young people to make informed decisions, develop positive habits, and achieve their goals.

This guide is designed to provide practical advice and insights on how to guide the next generation. We will explore effective communication strategies, provide guidance on sensitive issues such as mental health and drugs, and discuss how to balance freedom and responsibility. By following these tips and techniques, you can help shape the future by nurturing and empowering the next generation of leaders, thinkers, and innovators

Importance of guiding the next generation

Guiding the next generation is of utmost importance as it lays the foundation for the future of society. The youth of today are the leaders and decision-makers of tomorrow, and they need guidance and support to reach their full potential. Here are some reasons why guiding the next generation is so important:

Building a strong society: The next generation will be responsible for building and maintaining our society. It is important to guide them in a positive direction so that they can contribute to the growth and development of society. When the youth are guided to become responsible, compassionate and productive members of society, they will be able to contribute to building a strong and thriving community.

Ensuring a better future: Guiding the next generation is essential for ensuring a better future. By providing them with the necessary skills and knowledge, they will be equipped to handle the challenges of the future. They will be able to adapt to changing circumstances, make informed decisions and contribute to the progress of society.

Encouraging personal growth: Guiding the next generation is an opportunity to encourage personal growth and development. It allows them to explore their interests and passions, develop their skills and talents, and become confident and self-assured individuals. This, in turn, will help them achieve their goals and aspirations.

Transmitting values and traditions: Guiding the next generation is important for transmitting important values and traditions from one generation to the next.

By passing on cultural and moral values, we can ensure that they are not lost with time. This will help to preserve the rich cultural heritage of our society.

Preventing negative behavior: Guiding the next generation can also help to prevent negative behavior such as drug abuse, violence, and crime. By providing them with positive role models and guidance, we can help them make healthy and responsible choices.

guiding the next generation is crucial for building a strong society, ensuring a better future, encouraging personal growth, transmitting values and traditions, and preventing negative behavior. It is our responsibility as adults to provide them with the necessary guidance, support and resources they need to succeed. By doing so, we can help shape the future of our society and create a better world for generations to come.

Overview of the guide

Guiding teenagers can be a challenging yet rewarding experience. It is important to remember that teenagers are going through a time of significant change and development, both physically and emotionally. Here are some tips on how to effectively guide teenagers:

Build a relationship of trust: Teenagers need to trust their adult role models to feel comfortable sharing their thoughts and feelings. Take time to listen to them without judgement and show empathy towards their concerns.

Communicate clearly: Clear communication is essential when guiding teenagers. Be honest and direct in your communication and use age-appropriate language to explain complex ideas.

Set clear boundaries: Teenagers need structure and clear boundaries to help them navigate the world. Establish clear rules and expectations and consistently enforce them.

Be a positive role model: Teenagers often look up to their adult role models, so it's essential to model positive behaviours and attitudes.

Provide opportunities for growth: Encourage teenagers to take on new challenges and pursue their interests. Provide them with opportunities to explore their passions and develop new skills.

Address problematic behaviour: When teenagers engage in problematic behaviour, it is essential to address it in a non-judgmental way. Help them understand the consequences of their actions and provide guidance on how to make better choices in the future.

Celebrate successes: Celebrate the successes of teenagers and recognize their achievements, no matter how small they may be. This can help build confidence and motivation.

Overall, guiding teenagers requires patience, understanding, and empathy. By providing them with support, positive role models, and opportunities for growth, we can help them navigate the challenges of adolescence and become confident, responsible adults.

II.understanding the Next Generation

Understanding the Next Generation requires taking into account various factors that shape their experiences, values, and attitudes. These factors include technological advancements, globalisation, environmental changes, demographic shifts, and cultural shifts.

Technology plays a significant role in shaping the experiences and behaviours of the Next Generation. Young people are growing up in a world where technology is integrated into every aspect of their lives, from social media to education and entertainment. They are also more connected and have access to a vast amount of information and resources.

Globalisation is another important factor that shapes the Next Generation. Young people are growing up in a world where cultures, economies, and societies are increasingly interconnected. They are exposed to different cultures, languages, and ideas, which can broaden their perspectives and shape their values.

Environmental changes are also significant for the Next Generation. They are growing up in a world where climate change and environmental degradation are major issues. They are more aware of the need to protect the environment and are often more concerned about sustainability and conservation.

Demographic shifts are also important to consider when understanding the Next Generation. Young people are growing up in a more diverse world, both in terms of race and ethnicity and in terms of family structures. They are more likely to have friends and family members from different backgrounds, which can shape their attitudes and beliefs.

Finally, cultural shifts are also important for understanding the Next Generation. They are growing up in a world where traditional gender roles and social media. Understanding this group is important for many reasons, including business strategy, education, and social policy.

Some key characteristics of the Next Generation include:

Digital natives: They have grown up with technology and are comfortable using it for communication, entertainment, and work.

Socially conscious: They are concerned about social and environmental issues, and are often more willing to support companies and brands that share their values.

Diverse: They come from a wide range of ethnic, cultural, and socioeconomic backgrounds, and are more likely to embrace diversity and inclusivity.

Entrepreneurial: They are more likely to start their own businesses and pursue careers that allow them to be creative and independent.

Flexible: They are comfortable with change and are more likely to work in non-traditional ways, such as remote or freelance work.

Global: They have a wider worldview and are more likely to work, study, and travel internationally.

To understand and engage with the Next Generation, it's important to listen to their perspectives and experiences, and to be open to new ideas and ways of doing things. This means adapting to new technologies, promoting diversity and inclusion, and being mindful of social and environmental issues.

Characteristics of the current generation of teenagers

It is important to note that any broad generalisations about an entire generation should be taken with a grain of salt, as individuals within a generation can vary greatly in their beliefs, values, and behaviours. However, based on research and observations, here are some characteristics that may be associated with the current generation of teenagers, also known as Generation Z:

Digital natives: This generation has grown up with technology as an integral part of their lives, and they are generally comfortable with using smartphones, social media, and other digital tools.

Diversity and inclusivity: Generation Z is more diverse than previous generations, and they tend to be more accepting of different races, genders, sexual orientations, and other identities.

Activism: Many members of Generation Z are passionate about social justice issues and are willing to take action to create positive change in their communities and the world.

Mental health awareness: There is a growing awareness among teenagers about mental health and the importance of seeking help when needed. Many are vocal about mental health challenges and are advocating for more resources and support.

Entrepreneurial spirit: Generation Z is known for its entrepreneurial spirit, with many young people starting their own businesses or pursuing creative endeavours.

Delayed milestones: Some studies suggest that Generation Z is delaying certain milestones, such as getting a driver's licence, starting a job, or moving out of their parents' home, compared to previous generations.

Political engagement: Many teenagers in Generation Z are politically engaged and interested in the issues that affect their communities and the world at large.

It's worth noting that not all teenagers fit these characteristics, and individual differences and experiences can play a significant role in shaping one's beliefs, values, and behaviours.

Identifying common issues and challenges

identifying some common issues and challenges faced by teenagers. Here are a few examples:

Peer pressure: Teenagers often face pressure from their peers to conform to social norms, engage in risky behaviours, or try drugs or alcohol.

Bullying: Bullying is a common issue that many teenagers face, whether as a victim, a bystander, or a perpetrator.

Mental health: Teenagers may struggle with mental health issues, such as anxiety, depression, and stress. These issues can have a significant impact on their academic and social lives.

Self-esteem: Teenagers may struggle with self-esteem issues, which can be exacerbated by social media and the pressure to look and act a certain way.

Relationships: Teenagers may struggle to navigate romantic relationships, friendships, and family dynamics. They may also experience relationship problems, such as breakups or conflicts with friends or family members.

Academic pressure: Teenagers may feel pressure to perform well academically, especially if they plan to attend college. This pressure can cause stress and anxiety.

Identity and self-discovery: Teenagers may struggle with their sense of identity and self-discovery. They may be questioning their gender identity or sexual orientation or trying to find their place in the world.

Substance abuse: Teenagers may experiment with drugs or alcohol, which can lead to addiction and other health problems.

Technology addiction: Teenagers may become addicted to technology, spending excessive amounts of time on their phones, computers, or other devices.

Risky behaviours: Teenagers may engage in risky behaviours, such as driving under the influence, unprotected sex, or dangerous stunts, which can have serious consequences.

III. Effective Communication Strategies

Effective communication strategies for teenagers include the following:
Active listening: Teenagers often want to be heard and understood. Listening to them without interruption and showing empathy can go a long way in building trust and strengthening relationships.

Encourage open communication: Encourage teenagers to express themselves freely and openly without fear of judgement or punishment.

Use clear language: Use language that is clear, concise, and easy to understand. Avoid using complex vocabulary or talking down to them.

Be patient: Teenagers may take longer to process information and respond to questions. Being patient and giving them enough time to articulate their thoughts can help them feel heard and understood.

Provide feedback: Give feedback on what they have said or done, both positive and constructive. Acknowledge their efforts and offer suggestions for improvement where necessary.

Use humour: Humour can help to break the ice and create a relaxed atmosphere for communication.

Respect their privacy: Respect their need for privacy and personal space. Avoid prying or asking intrusive questions.

Use technology: Teenagers are often comfortable with technology and may prefer to communicate via text messages or social media. Use technology to stay in touch and communicate with them.

Be flexible: Be flexible in your communication style and be open to changing your approach to suit their needs.

Lead by example: Model good communication skills by being respectful, honest, and clear in your own communication with them.

Listening actively to teenagers

Active listening to teenagers involves a few key steps:

Give them your full attention: When teenagers are speaking to you, make sure to give them your full attention. This means putting away distractions such as phones or other devices and making eye contact.

Avoid interrupting: Resist the urge to interrupt or finish their sentences. Allow them to fully express themselves before responding.

Listen without judgement: Try to listen without judging or jumping to conclusions. Be open to hearing their point of view, even if you don't agree with it.

Paraphrase: Repeat what they have said in your own words to ensure that you understand their message correctly. This can also help them feel heard and understood.

Ask clarifying questions: If you are unsure about something they have said, ask clarifying questions to gain a better understanding of their perspective.

Validate their feelings: Validate their feelings by acknowledging how they feel, even if you don't agree with their actions or decisions.

Show empathy: Show empathy by putting yourself in their shoes and understanding how they may be feeling.

Summarise: At the end of the conversation, summarise what was discussed to ensure that you both have a clear understanding of the conversation.

By actively listening to teenagers, you can help build trust, strengthen relationships, and facilitate effective communication.

Building rapport and trust

Building rapport and trust with teenagers can be challenging but is essential for building a healthy and positive relationship with them. Here are some tips to help you build rapport and trust with teenagers:

Listen actively: Listen to what they have to say and show genuine interest in their thoughts, feelings, and opinions.

Be non-judgmental: Avoid being judgmental and try to understand their perspective. This helps create a sense of mutual respect and trust.

Be authentic: Be yourself and don't try to be someone you're not. This helps create a sense of trust and authenticity.

Establish boundaries: Establish clear boundaries and expectations for behaviour. This helps create a sense of safety and security.

Offer support: Offer support and guidance when they need it, but also encourage them to take responsibility for their actions and decisions.

Show appreciation: Acknowledge their efforts and achievements and show appreciation for their positive behaviour.

Respect their privacy: Respect their privacy and avoid prying into their personal lives unless it is necessary for their well-being.

Remember, building rapport and trust with teenagers takes time and effort. By consistently applying these tips, you can build a positive and trusting relationship with the teenagers in your life.

Using non-judgmental language

Using non-judgmental language with teenagers is important because it helps create a safe and respectful environment for communication. Here are some tips for using non-judgmental language with teenagers:

Use "I" statements: Use "I" statements to express your own feelings and experiences, rather than making assumptions or judgments about the teenager's behaviour or actions. For example, "I feel concerned when I see you smoking" instead of "You're making a bad choice by smoking."

Focus on behaviour: Focus on the behaviour itself, rather than labelling the teenager as "good" or "bad". For example, "I noticed that you didn't complete your homework" instead of "You're so lazy, you never do your homework."

Avoid labelling: Avoid using labels or generalisations to describe the teenager. For example, "You're always so messy" instead of "I noticed that your room is messy right now."

Be specific: Be specific about the behaviour or situation you want to address, and avoid making assumptions about the teenager's intentions or motivations. For example, "I noticed that you've been staying up late and missing school" instead of "You're just trying to avoid going to school."

Show empathy: Show empathy and understanding towards the teenager's perspective and feelings, and avoid being dismissive or invalidating. For example, "I can see that you're feeling really frustrated right now" instead of "You're overreacting."

Remember, using non-judgmental language takes practice and patience. By consistently applying these tips, you can communicate effectively and respectfully with teenagers

IV. Providing Support and Guidance

Providing support and guidance for teenagers can be challenging, but it is also very rewarding. Teenagers are going through a lot of changes in their lives, both physically and emotionally, and they often need someone to talk to and guide them through these changes. Here are some tips for providing support and guidance for teenagers:

Listen to them: One of the most important things you can do for a teenager is to listen to them. Give them your full attention, and don't interrupt or judge them. Let them express their feelings and concerns without fear of being criticised or dismissed.

Be available: Make yourself available to them when they need to talk. Let them know that you are there for them, and that they can come to you anytime they need support or guidance.

Respect their privacy: Teenagers value their privacy, so make sure you respect it. Don't pry into their personal lives or force them to share information they are not comfortable sharing.

Offer guidance, not judgement: When offering guidance, try to be non-judgmental. Teenagers are still learning and growing, and they need guidance to help them make good decisions. Instead of criticising or punishing them for mistakes, offer constructive advice on how they can improve.

Empathise with them: Teenagers often feel misunderstood, so it's important to empathise with them. Try to see things from their perspective, and validate their feelings and experiences.

Be a positive role model: As a role model, your behaviour can have a significant impact on a teenager's life. Show them how to be respectful, responsible, and compassionate by modelling those behaviours yourself.

Help them build self-esteem: Teenagers are often self-conscious and insecure, so help them build their self-esteem by praising their accomplishments and encouraging their interests and talents.

Encourage healthy habits: Help teenagers develop healthy habits, such as exercise, good nutrition, and good sleep habits. Encourage them to avoid unhealthy behaviours, such as smoking, drugs, and alcohol.

By providing support and guidance for teenagers, you can help them navigate the challenges of adolescence and develop into happy, healthy adults.

Creating a supportive environment

Providing support and guidance for teenagers can be challenging, but it is also very rewarding. Teenagers are going through a lot of changes in their lives, both physically and emotionally, and they often need someone to talk to and guide them through these changes. Here are some tips for providing support and guidance for teenagers:

Listen to them: One of the most important things you can do for a teenager is to listen to them. Give them your full attention, and don't interrupt or judge them. Let them express their feelings and concerns without fear of being criticised or dismissed.

Be available: Make yourself available to them when they need to talk. Let them know that you are there for them, and that they can come to you anytime they need support or guidance.

Respect their privacy: Teenagers value their privacy, so make sure you respect it. Don't pry into their personal lives or force them to share information they are not comfortable sharing.

Offer guidance, not judgement: When offering guidance, try to be non-judgmental. Teenagers are still learning and growing, and they need guidance to help them make good decisions. Instead of criticising or punishing them for mistakes, offer constructive advice on how they can improve.

Empathise with them: Teenagers often feel misunderstood, so it's important to empathise with them. Try to see things from their perspective, and validate their feelings and experiences.

Be a positive role model: As a role model, your behaviour can have a significant impact on a teenager's life. Show them how to be respectful, responsible, and compassionate by modelling those behaviours yourself.

Help them build self-esteem: Teenagers are often self-conscious and insecure, so help them build their self-esteem by praising their accomplishments and encouraging their interests and talents.

Encourage healthy habits: Help teenagers develop healthy habits, such as exercise, good nutrition, and good sleep habits. Encourage them to avoid unhealthy behaviours, such as smoking, drugs, and alcohol.

By providing support and guidance for teenagers, you can help them navigate the challenges of adolescence and develop into happy, healthy adults.

Encouraging healthy habits and positive behaviours

Encouraging healthy habits and positive behaviours in teenagers can be a challenging task, but it is essential for their overall well-being and future success. Here are some strategies that may help:

Be a role model: As an adult, your actions and behaviours can have a significant impact on the behaviour of teenagers around you. So, it's essential to model healthy habits and positive behaviours that you want them to adopt.

Educate them: Educate teenagers on the importance of healthy habits like regular exercise, good nutrition, and sufficient sleep. Also, provide them with information about the negative consequences of unhealthy behaviours like smoking, alcohol consumption, and drug use.

Encourage physical activity: Encourage teenagers to participate in sports, go for a walk, or engage in any other physical activity they enjoy. Physical activity not only helps maintain physical health but also helps manage stress and improve mental health.

Provide healthy food choices: Provide healthy food options and encourage them to choose nutritious foods over junk food. This can help them develop a healthy relationship with food and promote good eating habits.

Set rules and boundaries: Set reasonable rules and boundaries, such as setting a curfew or limiting screen time. This helps teenagers develop discipline and responsibility while protecting them from negative influences.

Encourage positive social interactions: Encourage teenagers to engage in positive social interactions with their peers and adults. This can help them build healthy relationships and develop good communication skills.

Praise positive behaviour: Acknowledge and praise positive behaviour, such as making healthy choices, being responsible, and showing empathy. This reinforces positive behaviours and encourages teenagers to continue making good choices.

Remember, it takes time and patience to develop healthy habits and positive behaviours. As a parent, caregiver, or role model, your support and encouragement can make a significant difference in helping teenagers make positive choices for their future.

Addressing sensitive issues such as mental health, drugs, and sex

Addressing sensitive issues such as mental health, drugs, and sex can be challenging, but it is crucial to have open and honest conversations with teenagers to promote their well-being and safety. Here are some strategies that may help:

Create a safe and supportive environment: When addressing sensitive topics, it's essential to create a safe and supportive environment where teenagers feel comfortable to share their thoughts and feelings without fear of judgement or criticism.

Educate yourself: Educate yourself about the issues you want to discuss with teenagers, so you can provide accurate and relevant information.

Start early: Start talking about these topics early before teenagers start facing the challenges of peer pressure and other external influences.

Use age-appropriate language: Use age-appropriate language that teenagers can understand and avoid using medical jargon or technical terms that may confuse or intimidate them.

Listen actively: Active listening is essential to understand teenagers' perspectives and feelings, and help them feel heard and validated.

Normalise the conversation: Normalise the conversation by emphasising that the

issues you are discussing are common and
natural, and that seeking help or support is
a sign of strength.

Encourage open communication:
Encourage open communication and
establish a regular check-in to monitor how
teenagers are doing and address any
concerns they may have.

Remember, addressing sensitive issues with
teenagers requires sensitivity, empathy, and
respect for their feelings and experiences.
It's essential to create a safe and supportive
environment that encourages open
communication and helps teenagers feel
heard and valued.

V. Balancing Freedom and Responsibility

Balancing freedom and responsibility is an important aspect of parenting and raising teenagers. Teenagers need a certain degree of freedom to explore their interests, make their own choices, and develop independence, but they also need to learn responsibility and accountability for their actions. Here are some tips for balancing freedom and responsibility for teenagers:

Set clear expectations: Communicate your expectations and rules clearly with your teenager. Make sure they understand the consequences of breaking rules, and that you will hold them accountable for their actions.

Encourage open communication: Create an open and non-judgmental environment where your teenager can talk to you about their concerns and experiences. This will help them feel comfortable discussing their decisions with you and seeking your guidance when needed.

Give age-appropriate freedom: Provide your teenager with age-appropriate freedom to make decisions and explore their interests. This will help them develop a sense of independence and responsibility. However, it's important to set limits and boundaries to ensure their safety and well-being.

Encourage responsibility: Teach your teenager the importance of responsibility and accountability. Give them age-appropriate chores and responsibilities at home, and encourage them to take ownership of their actions.

Model responsible behaviour: As a parent, it's important to model responsible behaviour. Show your teenager how to make responsible decisions and follow through on commitments. This will help them understand the importance of responsibility and how it can impact their lives.

Provide guidance and support: Offer guidance and support to your teenager as they navigate the challenges of adolescence. Encourage them to ask for help when needed, and provide resources and support to help them make responsible decisions.

Balancing freedom and responsibility is an ongoing process, and it's important to adjust your approach as your teenager grows and develops. By providing your teenager with age-appropriate freedom and responsibility, setting clear expectations, and offering guidance and support, you can help them develop the skills and confidence they need to become responsible and independent adults.

Setting boundaries and expectations

Setting boundaries and expectations is an important part of parenting teenagers. Adolescence is a time when young people are learning to become more independent, while still needing guidance and support from their parents. Here are some tips for setting boundaries and expectations with your teenager:

Be clear and consistent: Make sure your expectations are clear and that you are consistent in enforcing them. This will help your teenager know what is expected of them and what the consequences will be if they do not meet those expectations.

Involve your teenager: Involve your teenager in setting boundaries and expectations. This will help them feel like they have a say in the rules and will be more likely to follow them. It can also help them develop decision-making and problem-solving skills.

Focus on safety: Set boundaries and expectations that prioritise safety, such as curfews, rules about driving, and guidelines for internet use. These rules should be non-negotiable and consistently enforced.

Allow for independence: While it's important to set boundaries, it's also important to allow your teenager some independence. This can help them develop self-confidence and decision-making skills. Consider allowing them to make some decisions on their own, such as choosing their own clothes or deciding how to spend their free time.

Be flexible: While consistency is important, it's also important to be flexible when appropriate. If your teenager shows responsibility and good judgement, consider easing up on some rules or adjusting them to better fit their needs.

Communicate: Keep the lines of communication open with your teenager. Listen to their concerns and be willing to compromise when necessary. This will help build a stronger relationship and foster trust between you and your teenager.

Remember that setting boundaries and expectations is not about controlling your teenager, but rather about helping them learn to make responsible decisions and keeping them safe. Be patient and understanding, and be willing to adjust your approach as your teenager grows and changes.

<u>Encouraging independence while maintaining guidance On teenagers</u>

Encouraging independence while maintaining guidance is a delicate balancing act that parents of teenagers must navigate. Here are some tips for striking the right balance:

Allow your teenager to make age-appropriate decisions: Give your teenager opportunities to make decisions that are appropriate for their age and level of maturity. This could include choosing their own clothes or deciding how to spend their allowance. When your teenager makes a decision, offer guidance and support, but allow them to take the lead.

Set clear boundaries and expectations: While it's important to give your teenager some freedom, it's equally important to set clear boundaries and expectations. This could include rules around curfew, homework, and chores. Make sure your teenager understands the rules and the consequences for breaking them.

Listen to your teenager: Encourage your teenager to express their thoughts and feelings, and listen to what they have to say. This will help them feel heard and valued, and can also help you understand their perspective. When you listen to your teenager, you can better guide them towards making responsible decisions.

Offer guidance and support: While it's important to let your teenager make their own decisions, it's equally important to offer guidance and support when they need it. For example, if your teenager is struggling with a school project, offer to help them brainstorm ideas or offer feedback on their work.

Allow natural consequences: When your teenager makes a mistake, allow them to experience the natural consequences of their actions. This can be a valuable learning experience, and can help them develop responsibility and self-awareness.

Be a positive role model: Your teenager is likely to model their behaviour after yours, so make sure you are setting a good example. Show your teenager how to make responsible decisions, communicate effectively, and handle conflicts in a constructive manner.

Remember, encouraging independence while maintaining guidance is a process that takes time and patience. Be supportive of your teenager as they navigate the challenges of adolescence, and offer guidance and support along the way. With your help, your teenager can develop the skills they need to become responsible and independent adults.

<u>Teaching decision-making skills</u>
Teaching decision-making skills to teenagers is important for their personal and academic development. Here are some steps you can take to teach decision-making skills to teenagers:

Involve them in decision-making: Involve teenagers in decision-making processes, such as family decisions or school decisions. This helps them understand the decision-making process and how it works.

Use relatable examples: Use real-life and relatable examples to explain the decision-making process. For example, using a decision about what to wear for a date, or what extracurricular activity to join.

Encourage critical thinking: Encourage teenagers to think critically about the information they gather and the options they consider. Ask questions to help them analyse the situation and weigh the pros and cons of each option.

Discuss consequences: Discuss the consequences of different decisions with teenagers. Help them understand how each decision can impact their lives and the lives of others.

Use role-playing: Use role-playing exercises to help teenagers practise decision-making skills. This can be a fun and engaging way to help them learn how to make informed decisions.

Encourage reflection: Encourage teenagers to reflect on the decisions they make and the outcomes of those decisions. Help them understand how they can learn from their decisions and use that knowledge to make better decisions in the future.

Provide positive feedback: Provide positive feedback when teenagers make good decisions. This reinforces their decision-making skills and encourages them to continue making good decisions.

Overall, teaching decision-making skills to teenagers requires patience, empathy, and a willingness to listen. By providing guidance and support, you can help teenagers develop the skills they need to make informed decisions and succeed in life.

VI. Role-Modeling and Leading by Example

Role-modelling and leading by example are important strategies for teaching teenagers how to make good decisions and develop positive values. Here are some ways to effectively use these strategies:

Practise what you preach: It is important to model the behaviours and values you want teenagers to adopt. For example, if you want teenagers to be respectful, you should model respectful behaviour towards them and others.

Be transparent: Be open and honest with teenagers about your own decision-making processes and the reasons behind your decisions. This can help them understand how to make informed decisions based on their values and goals.

Use positive language: Use positive language to encourage teenagers to adopt positive behaviours and values. For example, instead of saying "don't do drugs," say "stay healthy and make good choices."

Share stories: Share stories of people who have overcome adversity and made positive decisions. This can inspire teenagers to make positive choices in their own lives.

Encourage independence: Encourage teenagers to make their own decisions, while providing guidance and support. This can help them develop confidence and independence.

Provide opportunities for leadership: Provide opportunities for teenagers to lead and make decisions in their own lives, such as by giving them responsibility for planning a family event or leading a group project.

Provide feedback: Provide feedback when teenagers make positive decisions, and help them understand the consequences of

negative decisions. This can help them learn from their mistakes and make better decisions in the future.

Overall, role-modelling and leading by example can be powerful tools for teaching teenagers how to make good decisions and develop positive values. By providing guidance, support, and positive reinforcement, you can help teenagers become confident, responsible, and successful adults.

Being a positive influence for the next generation

Being a positive influence for the next generation is important for the future of society. Here are some ways to be a positive influence for the next generation:

Set a good example: Model the behaviour and values you want the next generation to emulate. This means being honest, respectful, compassionate, and responsible.

Listen and communicate: Take the time to listen to the next generation and communicate with them in a positive and supportive way. Encourage open and honest dialogue, and be willing to learn from them as well.

Provide guidance and support: Offer guidance and support when needed, while also encouraging the next generation to develop independence and make their own decisions.

Foster a love of learning: Encourage the next generation to develop a love of learning by providing opportunities for them to explore and discover new things. This can include exposing them to different cultures, experiences, and ideas.

Encourage creativity and critical thinking: Encourage the next generation to think creatively and critically, and to question the status quo. This can help them develop innovative solutions to problems and make positive changes in the world.

Be a mentor or role model: Offer mentorship or be a positive role model for the next generation. This can involve sharing your experiences, offering guidance, and being a source of inspiration and encouragement.

Practice kindness and empathy: Practice kindness and empathy towards the next generation and others. This can help them develop these important qualities as well, and create a more compassionate and caring society.

Overall, being a positive influence for the next generation requires patience, empathy, and a willingness to learn and grow together. By modelling positive behaviour and values, and offering guidance and support, we can help the next generation become confident, responsible, and successful individuals.

Demonstrating healthy behaviours and values

Demonstrating healthy behaviours and values to teenagers is important for their overall well-being and development. Here are some ways to effectively demonstrate healthy behaviours and values to teenagers:

Practice self-care: Take care of yourself physically, emotionally, and mentally. This can include eating healthy, getting enough sleep, exercising regularly, and managing stress.

Foster positive relationships: Model positive relationship skills, such as active listening, empathy, and effective communication. This can help teenagers develop healthy relationships with their peers and family members.

Promote healthy habits: Model healthy habits, such as regular exercise, healthy eating, and avoiding harmful substances. This can help teenagers develop lifelong healthy habits.

Demonstrate positive values: Model positive values, such as honesty, integrity, respect, responsibility, and compassion. This can help teenagers develop these values and integrate them into their own lives.

Encourage social responsibility: Encourage teenagers to take responsibility for their actions and make positive contributions to their communities. This can include volunteering, participating in community service, and supporting social justice causes.

Encourage growth mindset: Encourage teenagers to adopt a growth mindset, and to view mistakes as opportunities for growth and learning. This can help them develop resilience and a positive attitude towards challenges.

Provide positive feedback: Provide positive feedback when teenagers demonstrate healthy behaviours and values. This can reinforce these behaviours and values, and encourage teenagers to continue to make positive choices.

Overall, demonstrating healthy behaviours and values to teenagers requires consistent modelling, positive reinforcement, and a commitment to personal growth and development. By promoting healthy habits, fostering positive relationships, and encouraging social responsibility, we can help teenagers become healthy, responsible, and compassionate.

Encouraging social responsibility and civic engagement

Encouraging social responsibility and civic engagement in teenagers is essential to building a strong and responsible society. Here are some tips on how to encourage teenagers to be socially responsible and engaged in their communities:

Lead by example: As a parent, guardian, or role model, it's crucial to demonstrate social responsibility and civic engagement yourself. Let your teenager see you volunteering, donating to charity, or participating in community activities.

Educate them: Explain to teenagers the importance of social responsibility and civic engagement. Help them understand how their actions can impact their communities and the world at large.

Give them opportunities: Encourage teenagers to participate in community service, volunteer work, and other civic activities. Look for opportunities in your local area that align with your teenager's interests.

Support their passions: Help your teenager find a cause or issue that they're passionate about. Encourage them to get involved in advocacy and activism related to that issue.

Discuss current events: Talk to your teenager about current events and encourage them to form opinions and take action on issues that matter to them.

Foster critical thinking: Encourage teenagers to think critically about the world around them. Help them understand the root causes of social problems and think creatively about solutions.

Celebrate their contributions:
Recognize and celebrate your teenager's contributions to their community. This will help reinforce the importance of social responsibility and civic engagement.

Remember, the more teenagers become socially responsible and engaged in their communities, the more likely they are to become responsible and engaged adults who positively contribute to the family.

VII. Conclusion

in conclusion, guiding the next generation is an essential task for all of us, as we have a responsibility to prepare our youth to become responsible, productive, and compassionate adults. By providing positive role models, setting clear expectations, offering support and guidance, and fostering a sense of purpose and belonging, we can help the next generation develop the skills, values, and attitudes they need to succeed in life and make a positive impact in the world. We must encourage them to take risks, learn from failures, and strive for excellence while embracing their unique talents and individuality. Ultimately, it is up to all of us to work together to build a better future for the next generation, and it starts with investing in their development and well-being today

<u>Recap of key points</u>

here is a recap of the key points on guiding the next generation:

Provide positive role models: Children learn by example, so it's essential to model the behaviours and values you want to see in the next generation.

Set clear expectations: Establishing clear expectations and boundaries helps children develop self-discipline and responsibility.

Offer support and guidance: Encourage children to pursue their interests, offer guidance and support as needed, and provide opportunities for growth and development.

Foster a sense of purpose and belonging: Help children develop a sense of purpose and belonging by encouraging them to explore their passions and find ways to contribute to their communities.

Encourage risk-taking and learning from failure: Teach children to embrace challenges, take risks, and learn from failure as part of the learning process.

Strive for excellence while embracing individuality: Encourage children to strive for excellence while also embracing their unique talents and individuality.

Overall, guiding the next generation requires a combination of positive role modelling, clear expectations, support and guidance, a sense of purpose and belonging, risk-taking and learning from failure, and a balance between striving for excellence and embracing individuality. By investing in the development and well-being of the next generation today, we can build a brighter future for everyone.

Final thoughts on guiding the next generation

First and foremost, it is important to lead by example. Children learn by observing the behaviour of those around them, so it is crucial to model the behaviour that you want to see in them. This includes traits such as kindness, honesty, empathy, and responsibility.

Secondly, it is important to listen to and communicate with the next generation. They have their own unique perspectives and experiences, and it is important to hear them out and validate their feelings. Creating a safe and open environment for communication can help build trust and foster healthy relationships.

Thirdly, it is important to encourage independence and problem-solving skills. Giving children the tools they need to make decisions and solve problems on their own will help build confidence and self-reliance. This includes teaching them how to think critically, make informed decisions, and learn from mistakes.

Finally, it is important to instil a love of learning in the next generation. Encouraging curiosity and a thirst for knowledge can help them develop a growth mindset and a lifelong love of learning. This can involve exposing them to new experiences, encouraging them to ask questions, and supporting their interests and passions.

Overall, guiding the next generation requires patience, empathy, and a commitment to creating a safe and supportive environment that encourages growth and learning.